HEALTHY FOR LIFE

Food AND EATING

Anna Claybourne

W

Franklin Watts
Published in paperback in Great Britain in 2019 by The Watts Publishing Group

Credits
Series Editors: Sarah Peutrill and Sarah Ridley
Series Designer and Illustator: Dan Bramall
Cover Designers: Peter Scoulding and Cathryn Gilbert

Additional pictures by Shutterstock.com
Quorn™ is a registered trademark. See www.quorn.co.uk for more information.

Dewey number: 613.2
ISBN 978 1 4451 4971 4

Printed in China

MIX
Paper from
responsible sources
FSC® C104740
FSC
www.fsc.org

Franklin Watts
An imprint of
Hachette Children's Group
Part of The Watts Publishing Group
Carmelite House
50 Victoria Embankment
London EC4Y 0DZ
An Hachette UK Company
www.hachette.co.uk

www.franklinwatts.co.uk

CONTENTS

Food for life

Everyone needs food!

Like every other human being on the planet, you have a human body. Your body is constantly moving around, repairing itself and growing new parts, such as hair and fingernails. It also does all kinds of jobs, like seeing, thinking and breathing. To do all this, it needs a steady supply of fuel. And for your body, that fuel is food.

What does food do for you?

Food gives your body three main things:

FOOD

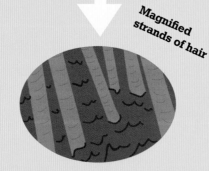

Magnified strands of hair

ENERGY

Just like a car burning engine fuel to make it move, your body gets energy from food. This makes your muscle cells work, so you can walk, talk, swim or dance.

Food also gives all your other cells the energy they need to work – whether they are brain cells, light-detecting cells in your eyes, or any other kind.

BUILDING BLOCKS

As well as moving, your body builds itself. It grows new hair, fingernails and skin all the time. If you have a cut or sore, your body repairs it. And if you aren't an adult yet, your whole body is growing bigger, too.

ESSENTIAL INGREDIENTS

Lastly, food is full of useful ingredients that your body needs in order to work. Iron is a great example. You only need a tiny bit, but it's essential for helping your blood to carry oxygen to all your cells. You get iron, and many other vital substances, from your food.

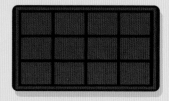

Pasta = full of energy!

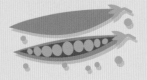

Peas = good for building!

Dark chocolate = a good source of iron!

A giant panda munches piles of bamboo shoots every day.

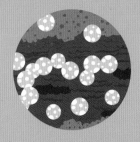

These toadstools feed on the rotting log they're growing on.

Tigers mainly eat other animals.

Who eats what?

It's not just humans who need food – all living things do.

A plant uses air, water and energy from sunlight to make food.

Humans are mostly omnivores, eating many different types of food.

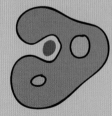

A tiny single-celled amoeba wraps itself around food.

Healthy, happy eating

However, food can be confusing. There's a lot of information out there about which foods are 'good' or 'bad' for you – and it seems to change every week! And people can sometimes get very stressed about food and eating, and how it affects their bodies.

This book explains how food works, so you can make your own decisions armed with all the facts.

What happens to food?

For most people, food is a big part of daily life. Most of us eat several meals a day, and maybe enjoy a few snacks too. You have special food at parties and celebrations. You might love cooking and trying out new recipes.

But once we've eaten our food, most of us stop thinking about it. While you get on with your day, what is your food actually doing?

Through the tube!

Your body has a system for dealing with food, called the digestive system. It's basically a long tube that carries food right through your body, taking in quite a few stops, twists and turns along the way. As food moves along, it changes – from the large, recognisable items you eat, into a mushy soup, broken down into the separate chemicals that make up food.

In the stomach, food breaks down into chyme (a sort of mushy soup).

That's because your body can't use 'whole' food to do its jobs. Your muscle cells need energy to work, for example – but muscle cells are tiny. They can't run on whole pieces of pasta. Instead, your body has to extract the useful bits, or 'nutrients', from food, and send them to the right places.

IN!

Time to eat!

Step 1: the mouth

You chew food up with your teeth and mix it with saliva (spit) to make it soft.

Step 2: the throat

You swallow, pushing lumps of food down your throat.

Step 3: the oesophagus

This tube carries chewed food down to your stomach.

Step 4: the stomach

Your stomach mixes food with strong acid to dissolve it.

Step 5: the small intestine

Your small intestine soaks up nutrients from the dissolved food. They move into your blood to be carried around the body.

Step 6: the large intestine

The large intestine collects leftover food that your body doesn't need.

OUT!

Lumps of waste, called faeces (or poo) get pushed out into the toilet.

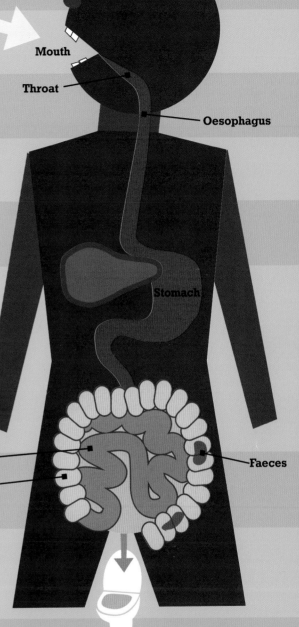

The small intestine is LONG – about four times your total height! It's tightly coiled up to fit inside you.

Mouth
Throat
Oesophagus
Stomach
Small intestine
Large intestine
Faeces

Body systems

The digestive system is just one of many systems your body uses to do different jobs. For example, your nervous system carries messages from your senses to your brain, and from your brain to your body. All the body systems, including the digestive system itself, need food to keep them working.

Food, energy and your body

We don't just need food – we need the right amount of food. This is especially true of the food that gives you energy. Too little, and you'll feel exhausted and worn out. Too much, and you won't be able to use all that energy up. Luckily, the body has a way of dealing with this.

Feast and famine

Long ago, before we had farms, shops and supermarkets, people had to hunt or gather their own food. Sometimes, there would be plenty – they would catch a woolly mammoth, or collect lots of nuts in the autumn. Sometimes, food would be scarce, and people might have to go without much to eat for days or even weeks.

The body copes with this by storing extra energy as extra body fat. If you take in more energy than you use up, you build up extra fat stores. (A healthy body already contains fat – this is just a bit extra.)

If you take in less energy than you use up, your body can get the energy it needs by using up some of its fat stores.

This brilliant device has helped humans survive for millions of years. It means that even when there's not a steady supply of energy from food, the body can even things out.

Calories

Calories are units used to measure how much energy there is in food.
Some foods contain lots of calories, and others hardly any – there's a huge range.

Here are a few calorie-rich, high-energy foods:

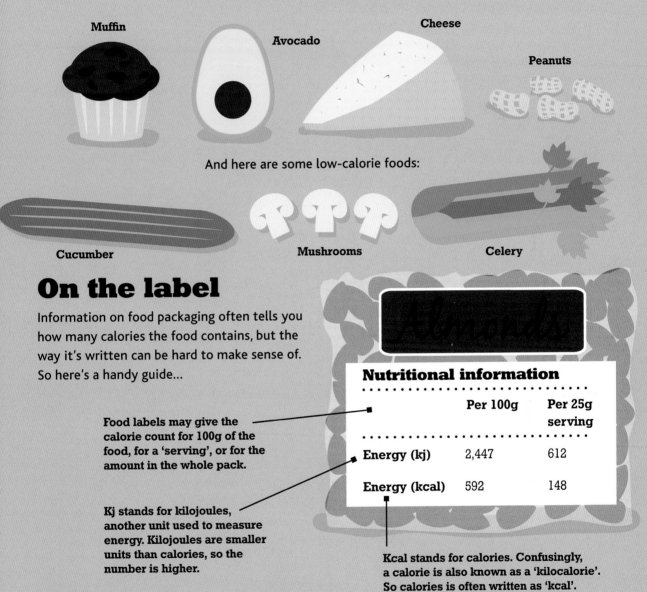

Muffin

Avocado

Cheese

Peanuts

And here are some low-calorie foods:

Cucumber

Mushrooms

Celery

On the label

Information on food packaging often tells you
how many calories the food contains, but the
way it's written can be hard to make sense of.
So here's a handy guide...

Almonds

Nutritional information

	Per 100g	Per 25g serving
Energy (kj)	2,447	612
Energy (kcal)	592	148

Food labels may give the
calorie count for 100g of the
food, for a 'serving', or for the
amount in the whole pack.

Kj stands for kilojoules,
another unit used to measure
energy. Kilojoules are smaller
units than calories, so the
number is higher.

Kcal stands for calories. Confusingly,
a calorie is also known as a 'kilocalorie'.
So calories is often written as 'kcal'.

Energy in and out

Your body uses up a certain number of calories every day. This varies a lot, depending on
things like your age and size, and whether you do lots of sport, walking or dancing. It also
takes energy to grow, so children and teenagers need calories for that, too.

If you take in more calories than you need, your body will gradually store the extra
energy as extra fat. If you take in less than you need, you will lose some of your body fat.

Food groups

As well as containing varying amounts of calories, foods can be divided into different types, or food groups, depending on the types of things they do for your body. To give your body all the different nutrients it needs, you need food from all the different groups. Luckily, that's not too difficult, as there are so many types of food!

This chart shows the food groups and some foods that contain them.

Of course, one food can contain nutrients from more than one food group. Pasta, for example, contains lots of carbohydrate, but also some protein. Salmon contains lots of protein, but also some essential fat.

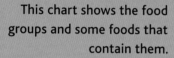

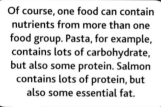

Fibre
Fibre helps your large intestine to work well, and can help keep your heart healthy too.

Minerals
Your body needs small amounts of minerals, like iron and calcium. For example, calcium, found in dairy foods and leafy vegetables, helps you build strong bones and teeth.

Vitamins
Vitamins are chemicals that help different body parts work. There are many vitamins, found in a wide range of foods. For example, vitamin C, found in potatoes and oranges, helps your body fight off illnesses.

Busting the fat myth

Fat is vital for your body, especially when you are still growing. However, the word 'fat' can also be used to describe a person who is carrying a lot of extra fat on their body – also known as being overweight.

Not surprisingly, this makes some people think that if you eat fat, you will become fat. But this isn't true at all. Taking in extra calories makes your body store fat, but those calories are just as likely to come from other foods, especially sugar.

Carbohydrates

Carbohydrates (or 'carbs') give you energy, and can be converted into body fat. They are found in stodgy or sugary foods.

Protein

Protein helps your body grow, build new parts and repair itself.

Some food manufacturers label food as '95 per cent fat-free', or 'low-fat', and market it as 'healthy'. In fact, this food could be quite unhealthy, if it contains a lot of sugar, for example.

Fats

All your cells need fats to work, especially brain cells. Your body also has a layer of fat that cushions your bones and keeps you warm. Some fats, such as those found in salmon, seeds and avocados, are especially useful for your body.

What's more, scientists have recently found that natural sources of fat – such as butter and olive oil – can be better for your body than some artificial or 'low-fat' alternatives.

There are lots of different 'healthy eating' messages – and many of them disagree with each other! It can be very hard to keep up with what's 'in' and what's 'out'. Here are just a few of the things that can create confusion.

Conflicting advice

Another problem is that foods may be healthy or unhealthy in different ways. For example, eating a lot of red meat isn't very good for your intestines. On the other hand, if you are anaemic (lacking in iron) you may be advised to eat red meat to help you take in more iron.

Changing stories

One problem is that we are always finding out more about how foods affect us. For example, people once thought a very low-fat diet was healthy. Some studies now suggest that too much sugar is more unhealthy than fat. But it can take time for the message to get through to everyone.

Milk

Butter

A lot of nonsense!

Even worse, you'll find all kinds of 'healthy eating' advice, especially online, that isn't based on any real scientific evidence! For example, some websites say it's a good idea to live on nothing but fruit juice. Anyone can write whatever they like on the Internet, but it doesn't mean it's true!

CONFUSED!?

No wonder!

In fact, there are just a few basic tips for healthy eating that most experts agree on...

Eat for your needs

Taking in roughly the amount of energy that you need helps you to stay healthy. Being guided by your body, and how hungry you feel, helps you to meet your body's needs properly.

Eat everything

The more different foods you eat, the more different nutrients, vitamins and minerals your body will get. (And the more foods you'll discover that you love!)

Eat real food

The closer a food is to its natural state, the more likely it is to contain useful nutrients. So, for example, a fresh apple is better for you than a processed apple pie with a long shelf life. Cooking from scratch using fresh ingredients is healthier than eating ready meals (though you may not always have time).

Which leads us to...

. . . .

80/20

Experts also say that aiming to eat healthily *most* of the time – around 80 per cent – is probably better than trying to be perfect and worrying non-stop about what you eat. After all, food is fun, and an important part of social occasions. It's normal to enjoy things like birthday cake, an ice cream at the seaside or the occasional junk food meal, rather than 'banning' any foods altogether.

Unhealthy eating

You might be wondering why healthy eating is important, and why we are always being told to do it. What happens if you don't eat healthily?

Missing out

Eating a narrow range of foods means you can miss out on important nutrients, vitamins or minerals – and that can make you ill.

No fruit or vegetables

If you never ate fruit or vegetables, you'd be short of vitamins, especially vitamin C. A lack of vitamin C can cause an unpleasant disease called scurvy. You get aches and pains and blotchy skin, your teeth fall out and you feel exhausted and miserable.

Long ago, sailors on long sea journeys often got scurvy, but these days it's quite rare.

I wish we'd brought some lemons and limes on board!

Not enough protein

A lack of protein can cause fragile hair and nails, muscle weakness and tiredness. If you get a cut or injury, or a zit, it can take a long time to heal. For older adults, a lack of protein could lead to fractured bones.

Not enough fat

If there's not enough fat in your diet, your skin and hair might start to feel dry. You could have trouble concentrating or remembering things, as brain signals need fat to work well.

Not enough iron

Teenagers, especially girls, can suffer from a lack of iron. It can make you feel tired and irritable, short of breath, or dizzy when you stand up. You might look pale and have headaches too.

Junk food

'Junk food' means food that has a lot of calories without many useful nutrients. It includes many types of fast food, takeaways, prepackaged snacks and fizzy drinks, and you'll often hear that it's not good for you. But why?

Junk food is often fried in trans-fat, a type of processed fat that's not very good for your heart.

Junk food often contains a lot of added sugar – even in things like a burger bun.

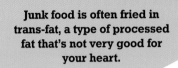

Processed foods, such as biscuits, are not fresh and contain a lot of hidden ingredients.

Large portions, such as big bakery items, can mean it's easy to take in more calories than you need.

Occasional junk food isn't a problem – but if you eat it all the time, you could end up short of nutrients, such as vitamin C or iron.

What's wrong with sugar?

Sugar is a natural food, and it contains useful calories, so why is it considered unhealthy? Scientists have found that eating a lot of sugar can cause several health problems:

! It damages teeth, leading to tooth decay.

! It can lead to a serious illness called type 2 diabetes.

! It can be addictive, especially if it's mixed with fat, meaning eating it makes you want to eat more.

! It can be easy to consume a lot of sugar without feeling very full – so you end up having many more calories than you need.

How heavy you are – your weight – is normally affected by what you eat. Taking in more energy than you need will add weight as you store extra body fat. Taking in less will reduce your weight, as you use up fat.

Weight can also be affected by certain illnesses, body chemicals called hormones, and by how 'well-built' and muscly you are. However, food is an important factor.

Worrying about weight

People in our society tend to care a lot about how they look. Adverts and films often feature models and actors who are unusually slim, and people can be teased or bullied about their weight. So it's no wonder that a lot of people worry about it – even when they are, in fact, perfectly healthy.

Overweight and underweight

Being very high in weight (overweight) or low in weight (underweight) can be unhealthy.

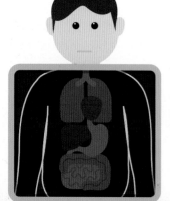

Being very overweight can increase the risk of illnesses such as diabetes and heart disease, and can cause back and leg problems.

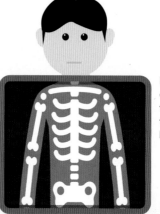

Being very underweight can make you very tired, and make it easier to catch bugs and break bones.

However, there isn't one perfect weight for everyone. In between being underweight and overweight, there's a wide range of healthy weights.

What is BMI?

You may have heard of BMI, short for Body Mass Index. It is a way of comparing your weight with your height to give a number. It gives a rough idea of whether your weight is healthy, high or low.

Low weight: **Height 1.5m**	**Weight 35kg**	**BMI: 15**
Healthy: **Height 1.5m**	**Weight 45kg**	**BMI: 19**
Healthy: **Height 1.5m**	**Weight 57kg**	**BMI: 24**
High weight: **Height 1.5m**	**Weight: 86kg**	**BMI: 37**

A large range of weights are within what the BMI system calls a 'healthy' weight.

However, BMI is a very simple measurement. It doesn't take account of your body shape, or how much of your weight is made of extra fat. You could have a high BMI because you are very muscly, for example.

So, if you are ever worried about your weight, it's best to ask a doctor about it. Don't just rely on BMI!

If you do want to work out your BMI, here's how:

1. Find your weight in kilograms.
2. Divide it by your height in metres.
3. Divide the answer by your height in metres again.

Diets

You've probably heard of people 'going on a diet' – sticking to a regime of special foods – often to lose weight. However, studies have shown diets aren't very good at controlling weight. They often change a person's weight for a while, then it changes back again. The more this happens, the more strain it puts on your body.

If your weight is unhealthy, according to a doctor, and you'd like to change it, it's more effective to change your eating habits permanently, to make them a bit healthier. For example, you could stop having junk food every day, and save it for special occasions.

I can't eat that!

There are millions of people who choose not to, or are not able to, eat certain foods. They may follow a special diet for all kinds of reasons...

Religious reasons

 Followers of Islam have strict rules about food. For example, they cannot eat pork.

 Followers of Judaism cannot eat pork, or any seafood except fish.

 Followers of Hinduism don't eat beef, and many are vegetarian.

Cutting out meat

Vegetarians don't eat meat or fish, but they may eat butter, cheese and eggs.

Vegans don't eat any animal products – no meat, fish, eggs, dairy or even honey.

A pescetarian eats fish, but not meat.

Health reasons

'Lactose-intolerant' people can't digest milk very well, so they eat a dairy-free diet.

You'll need a gluten-free diet if you're intolerant to gluten, found in wheat and some other grains. Some people have an illness called coeliac disease, which means gluten can make them very ill.

Food allergies are bad reactions to certain foods, such as nuts, eggs or seafood. Allergies can be dangerous, so you have to avoid the problem food.

Milk

Wheat

Prawn

Cashews

Checking labels

Sticking to some of these special diets can be really tricky. Processed foods often contain hidden animal products, gluten, dairy or nuts. You have to check the ingredients carefully!

Ingredients include:

pork gelatine

Chocolate mousse

Ingredients include:

milk powder

Ingredients include:

wheat gluten

Ingredients include:

eggs

Sliced bread

Soya sauce

Ice cream

Staying healthy

If one of these diets applies to you, how can you make sure you get the nutrients you need?

- Replace meat or fish with other protein – like an egg, a piece of cheese, or a meat alternative like Quorn™ or tofu.

- If you're going to someone's house and you're worried they won't have what you need, it's OK to take it with you – special gluten-free bread, for example.

- Snacks can be a good way to get nutrients. For example if you're a vegan, nuts such as almonds make a good snack as they contain protein, healthy fat and calcium.

- If you're eating out, call ahead to see if the restaurant can make something special for you, or check their menu online.

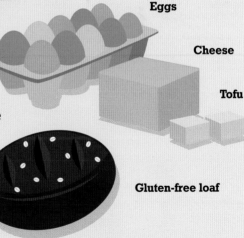

Eggs

Cheese

Tofu

Gluten-free loaf

Almonds

Healthy drinking

A typical human is between 60 and 70 per cent water. Water is essential for making all your cells work, and it makes up a large part of your blood. We need it to make saliva, tears and sweat, and we flush waste water out of our bodies in our breath and in our urine (wee). So it's essential to keep your water level topped up.

Hydrated and happy

Getting enough water is often called 'hydration' (from hydrogen, an element found in water). If you don't get enough, it's called being 'dehydrated' – and it can make you feel pretty bad...

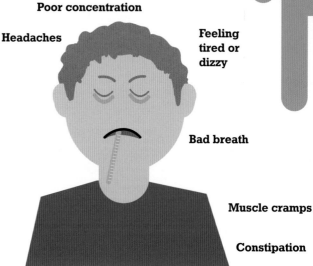

Poor concentration

Headaches

Feeling tired or dizzy

Bad breath

Muscle cramps

Constipation

How much hydration?

A typical person needs to take in about two litres of water a day. You'll need more if it's very hot, or you're playing sport and sweating a lot.

If you are getting enough water, you'll feel more energetic, your skin will look better, and you'll find it easier to focus on things.

However, you don't have to drink just plain water. There are plenty of ways to get the hydration you need.

Pure water
It is a good idea to drink a few glasses of pure water a day.

Milk
Milk is mostly water, and can be a healthy drink (as long as you aren't lactose-intolerant, or a vegan).

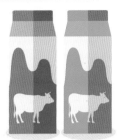

Tea
A cup of tea, especially if it's not too strong, will hydrate you well.

Food
Many foods contain lots of water.

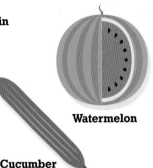

Sparkling water
If you don't like the taste of water much, you might prefer fizzy water sometimes instead.

Soup

Watermelon

Cucumber

Less healthy drinks

Besides water, some drinks contain other things that are less good for you.

Fizzy, sugary drinks
These contain lot of sugar, but they don't make you feel full up, so it's easy to have too much.

Hot chocolate, creamy iced drinks and milkshakes
These can also contain more sugar and calories than you need, especially if they come in large servings.

Coffee, cola and energy drinks
These contain a drug called caffeine. It can help you feel awake – but too much can make you jittery, and unable to get to sleep.

Diet drinks
These drinks contain sweeteners instead of sugar. That does mean they are less sugary and less full of calories – but they also contain more artificial chemicals, and are not as healthy as normal water.

Fruit juice
Fruit juice does contain water and some useful vitamins, but it's very sugary too.

Another problem with sugary drinks is that the sugar flows past your teeth and can cause tooth decay.

Eating disorders

We all need food, and often enjoy it, too. However, food can be an emotional subject, and some people worry about it a lot. Sometimes, anxiety and stress about food can become an eating-related illness, known as an eating disorder.

Three well-known eating disorders are:

Anorexia nervosa

The word 'anorexia' means loss of appetite, and 'nervosa' means nervous or anxious. So this illness, often just called anorexia, is about anxiety and emotions making you not want to eat. Sufferers may go without food for long periods, or try to throw up what they have eaten. They often lose a lot of weight and may feel very ill, tired or faint.

Bulimia nervosa

Also known as just bulimia, this illness makes you want to eat a lot, then try to vomit it up or go without food for a while. Sufferers swing between bingeing (eating as much food as they can) and starving. They often stay a normal weight overall, meaning bulimia can be hidden from others more easily.

Binge-eating disorder

This disorder, sometimes called BED for short, makes you want to eat a large amount of food, often in a very short time. Sufferers do not do this because they are hungry, but because they feel emotionally compelled to eat. Sometimes it happens at night when the person is half-asleep, and they don't even remember much about it.

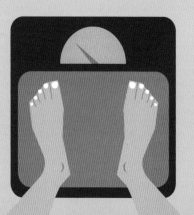

What causes eating disorders?

Some sufferers of anorexia feel that there is a lot of pressure on them to be thin, leading to a desire not to eat.

But eating disorders can have other causes too, which are not completely understood. They can occur when people feel out of control in their own lives, or very upset about something. Focusing on food can give them a distraction or a way of feeling in control. Some eating disorders also seem to run in families.

What can you do?

Eating disorders can be overwhelming, upsetting or frightening. People often want to hide their symptoms. They may feel ashamed, even though these disorders are illnesses like any other, and you can't help it if you have one.

If you're worried that you, or someone you know, may have an eating disorder, it's best to talk to a doctor, or an adult you trust, so that they can help.

Sports coach

Doctor or school nurse

Teacher

Grandparent

Parent

The good news is, there is lots of help available, and it's possible to recover from all types of eating disorder and go on to have a happy relationship with food.

Food safety

Preparing and making food yourself is a great way to eat healthily, be in charge of what you eat and save money too. But to avoid disasters, it has to be prepared, cooked and stored safely. Here are a few useful things you need to know...

Food poisoning

Some food, especially meat, can contain harmful germs before it's cooked.

- Chicken, pork, seafood and minced meat should be cooked until it's well-done right through.

- Knives, chopping boards and anything else that has touched the raw meat, as well as your hands, should be washed with soap and hot water straight away.

Washing food

Some food needs washing before eating – and some doesn't!

- Leafy vegetables such as leeks, spinach and lettuce should be washed before eating to get any soil out.
- It's best to wash the outsides of fruit and vegetables such as cucumbers and apples if you're eating the skin.

Eating apple peel is a great idea as it's full of fibre and nutrients!

- BUT... raw meat should never be washed, as this can splash germs around your kitchen. Yuck!

Storing food safely

- If you want to keep leftovers, they should be put in the fridge as soon as possible. Leaving fresh food at room temperature helps germs to grow.
- This is especially true for rice and pasta. Rice and pasta salad should always be kept cold, not lukewarm.

If it has sat in the sun all day, it's not safe to eat!

Use-by dates

Use-by dates on food are there to let you know how long the food will last, and when it might start to go off.

But if it says

BEST BEFORE:

– that means it might go a bit stale after the date, but could still be edible for a while.

If it says

USE BY:

– it means don't eat it after that date.

Use your senses!

Nature gave you a nose that's very good at detecting when food is rotten. It's how our ancestors stayed safe from the worst food poisoning germs.

If food smells off, disgusting and gross, it probably is! Even if it's still before the use-by date, you don't have to eat it.

You can also sometimes see mould growing on food – meaning it needs to be binned.

Enjoy your food!

Food is your friend. It's what keeps your body going, day after day, so that you can get on with being who you are and achieving what you want to achieve.

And on top of that, once you find the foods you love, eating can be one of the most enjoyable things in life. It's a way to get friends together, create something satisfying and experience new and interesting flavours.

If you want to become a chef, cookbook writer or farmer, food could even be your career!

Trying new foods

There's a whole world of food out there. Thanks to recipe books, restaurants and the wide range of ingredients in the shops, it's easy to try food from all kinds of cultures and traditions different from your own. Give them a go whenever you can, and you'll discover a wider range of foods you like.

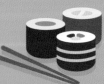

Thai curry

Salami

Empanada

Croissant

Sushi

Dumplings

Learning to cook

Being able to prepare your own food gives you control, choice and creativity. It doesn't have to be difficult – just a few key skills will allow you to make all kinds of things...

Pasta with sauce

Veggie curry

Banana muffins

Home-made burgers

If you want to learn to cook, or learn new things, one way is to ask a good cook you know to teach you their favourite recipes. There are also loads of great books, websites and blogs to help you.

Healthy habits

It can sometimes be really difficult to eat a wide range of things — for example, if the takeaway you visit with friends at lunchtime only sells junk food. But you can build other foods into your routine — for example by having some fruit on your breakfast, nuts for a snack or taking a turn to cook from scratch at home.

Quick fixes

You don't even need to be able to actually cook to make something great to eat.

Tortilla wrap + hummus + cucumber =

Salad leaves + avocado + mozzarella cheese + olives =

Toasted bagel + cream cheese + smoked salmon + sliced gherkin =

ENJOY!

Food groups guide

Food group	What it does for your body		Good sources
Carbohydrates (carbs)	Provides energy for muscles and other body parts		Bread, pasta, rice, oats, corn (maize), millet, peas, beans, lentils, couscous, fruit, breakfast cereals
Protein	Used to build and repair body tissues		Meat, fish, eggs, cheese, beans, lentils, nuts, seeds, yoghurt, tofu, Quorn™
Fat	Protects organs, stores energy, helps brain and nerves to work, keeps hair and skin supple		Olive oil, butter, avocados, oily fish like salmon and mackerel, nuts, seeds, eggs
Fibre	Keeps intestines healthy, good for your heart		Nuts, seeds, brown rice, oats, wholegrain bread, fruit and vegetables (especially with the skin on), beans, lentils, chickpeas

Vitamins and minerals:

Vitamin	What it does for your body		Good sources
Vitamin A	Helps keep eyes, heart and lungs working, helps fight off illnesses		Milk, cheese, eggs, oily fish, yogurt
B vitamins (8 types)	Help cells grow, help turn food into energy		Eggs, fish, seafood, green vegetables, mushrooms
Vitamin C	Keeps teeth and gums healthy, helps fight off germs		Citrus fruits, potatoes, peppers, berries, sprouts
Vitamin D	Helps build strong bones, helps fight off diseases		Oily fish, eggs (and also sunlight)
Vitamin E	Keeps cells in good condition		Nuts, plant oils, avocados
Vitamin K	Helps build bones and heal injuries		Broccoli, parsley, green leafy vegetables

Mineral	What it does for your body	Good sources
Iron	Helps blood carry oxygen, helps cells grow	Red meat, seafood, nuts, tofu, dark chocolate, apricots
Calcium	Helps build bones and teeth, helps muscles and nerves work	Milk, yoghurt, cheese, tofu, spinach, rhubarb
Copper	Helps form blood, fight germs and turn food into energy	Seafood, dark chocolate, nuts, seeds, mushrooms
Zinc	Helps build body parts, helps fight off illnesses	Meat, seafood, nuts
Potassium	Helps cells work, especially brain and nerve cells	Sweet potatoes, bananas, oranges, dates, raisins
Sodium	Helps balance liquids in the body, keeps cells healthy	Found in salt and salty foods (many people eat too much salt)
Phosphorus	Helps form DNA and bones; helps turn food into energy	Milk, cheese, yoghurt, eggs

Store cupboard basics list

This list of basic, long-lasting foods and flavourings will give you
what you need to turn all kinds of fresh ingredients into tasty meals.

Olive oil

Sunflower oil

Vinegar

Salt

Pepper

Herbs: basil, oregano, thyme, mint, parsley, tarragon

Spices: cinnamon, chilli powder, cumin, nutmeg, garam masala, turmeric

Stock cubes or stock powder

Garlic purée

Tomato purée

Lemon juice

Chilli sauce

Mustard

Plain flour

Cornflour

Brown sugar

Honey

Baking powder

Bicarbonate of soda

Glossary

allergy A bad reaction to a particular type of food, which can make some people very ill.

anaemic Having a lack of iron in your body, which makes your blood work less well.

anorexia nervosa (also called anorexia) An eating disorder that makes people want to avoid eating.

BED (binge-eating disorder) An eating disorder that makes people want to overeat.

BMI (Body Mass Index) A measurement found by comparing weight to height.

bulimia nervosa (also called bulimia) An eating disorder that makes people switch between eating too little, and eating too much, or eating too much and being sick.

calories Units used to measure the amount of energy contained in food.

carbohydrates (carbs) A type of food nutrient that gives the body energy.

coeliac disease A disease in which people have difficulty digesting gluten, found in wheat.

dehydration Not having enough water in your body.

diabetes An illness that makes it hard for the body to control the amount of sugar in the blood.

digestive system A series of organs and tubes that carry food through the body and break it down into nutrients.

DNA (deoxyribonucleic acid) The material found in all living cells which carries the information about how a living thing will look and function.

eating disorder A type of mental illness that affects how and what people want to eat.

faeces The scientific name for poo.

fat A type of nutrient that helps protect the body and helps brain cells to work.

fibre Parts of food that help the large intestine work smoothly and which absorb unhealthy fats, such as cholesterol, helping heart health.

food poisoning Various types of illness caused by eating food that has not been properly cooked or stored, or has 'gone off' – allowing germs to multiply.

gluten A type of protein found in wheat and some other cereals.

gluten-free A special diet people follow to avoid eating gluten.

hydration Getting enough water into your body.

junk food Food that is often high in calories, sugar and salt, but has not much other nutritional value.

kilocalories (kcal) Used on food packaging as another name for calories.

kilojoules (kj) Units used to measure the amount of energy contained in food.

lactose-intolerant Being unable to digest milk and dairy products well.

minerals Natural, non-living substances, such as iron and calcium, that are found in foods and are essential for the body in small amounts.

nutrients The chemicals found in food that give your body what it needs to work and grow.

oesophagus The tube that carries food down from your throat to your stomach.

omnivore A person or animal that eats both plant-based and animal-based foods.

pescetarian Someone who does not eat meat, but does eat fish.

processed food Food that has had a lot of changes made to it or additives put into it.

protein A type of nutrient that helps the body to grow new cells and repair damage.

Quorn™ A well-known mycoprotein, a vegetarian protein made from a type of fungi.

saliva Another name for spit.

scurvy A dangerous illness caused by a lack of vitamin C.

trans-fats A type of solid fat that can be made by processing some types of oil.

urine The scientific name for wee.

vegan Someone who does not eat meat or dairy or any other animal products.

vegetarian Someone who does not eat meat or fish.

. . . .

Food and recipe books

Go Faster Food for Kids: Top Nutrition Advice for Active Children with 101 Irresistible Recipes
by Kate Percy, 2013

How to Cook: Over 200 essential recipes to feed yourself, your friends & family
by Annie Bell, 2015

Cooking Up A Storm: The Teen Survival Cookbook
by Sam Stern, 2014

Teen Cuisine
by Matthew Locricchio, 2014

Websites

Go, Slow and Whoa! A Kid's Guide to Healthy Eating
kidshealth.org/en/kids/go-slow-whoa.html

BBC Good Food: Healthy Kids: Recipes
www.bbcgoodfood.com/recipes/collection/healthy-kids

TeensHealth: Eating Disorders
kidshealth.org/en/teens/eat-disorder.html

CYH Teen Health: Eating Well and Feeling Good
www.cyh.com/HealthTopics/HealthTopicDetails.aspx?p=243&id=2162&

Note to parents and teachers: Every effort has been made by the Publishers to ensure that these websites are suitable for children, that they are of the highest educational value, and that they contain no inappropriate or offensive material. However, because of the nature of the Internet, it is impossible to guarantee that the contents of these sites will not be altered. We strongly advise that Internet access is supervised by a responsible adult.

Index